COSTUME CAMEOS 3

by
Hazel Ulseth & Helen Shannon

TABLE OF CONTENTS

Published by **HOBBY HOUSE PRESS, INC.**
Cumberland, Maryland

Bonnets
and
Hats
1880s

ABOUT COSTUME CAMEOS 3

By this time our *Costume Cameos* need but little introduction; their origin, our little brain children, was discussed briefly in two previous issues. However, we will note for the as yet uninitiated that there are two *Costume Cameos* (1 and 2) preceding this. The first, a reprint from a very early issue, contains a delightful adaptation of a little girl's doll pattern from 1887, a skirt with bretelles, a Scottish hat and a cape with a choice of a hood or of two collars, along with lots of sewing hints including cartridge pleating.

Costume Cameos 2 has a pattern for a really lovely dress, full-skirted with gathered waist and lace-trimmed double bretelles, a beautiful bonnet and shoes, all for a 19in (48.3cm) doll. Along with this, lots of other goodies include patterns for tiny sitting teddy bears, and for old-fashioned paper dolls.

In this issue a slightly different format has been used; patterns are given for two different bonnets, a Poke bonnet in two sizes and a Normandy bonnet in two sizes.

Every effort has been made to insure that the would-be milliner will complete the bonnet project successfully on her own. Naturally we include our usual complement of added values in the form of more help with making ruching for bonnet trim, along with proper techniques for gluing, some "GLIMPSES of the PAST" in the form of old advertisements, and, would you believe it, much more!

Throughout this pattern specific references will be made to pages in *Antique Children's Fashions, 1880-1900, A Handbook for Dolls Costumers* by Hazel Ulseth and Helen Shannon, for detailed information about some of the sewing techniques used in the construction of these bonnets.

Illustration 1. 15in (38.1cm) Jumeau wearing a Poke bonnet. Note the simple trim of six-strand embroidery thread crocheted in a chain applied around the brim and tiny velour flowers laid in a narrow band. *Photograph by Marty Ulseth.*

Illustration 2. 12in (35.6cm) Belton wearing a Poke bonnet with double ruching trim and a band of tiny flowers. *Photograph by Marty Ulseth.*

BONNETS: Fit, Fabric and Furbelows

From times long past little girls have been enchanted with doll hats and bonnets. Paper doll sets always included cunning little hats in their gay lithographed color, commerical dolls had their flamboyant organdy bonnets with towering brims, and French bébés had their lovely creations of buckram, wire, ribbon and feathers reflecting the styles of the period.

Bonnets, like shoes, were not anchored and thus often disappeared over the passing years; or because they could be easily removed, suffered from wear and tear as little hands played with them constantly.

In addition to commercially-made headgear, there were, of course, an infinite variety of bonnets and hats made by loving mothers and grandmothers who bought dolls dressed in simple chemises, and created lovely wardrobes for them, or they made up dolls from the kits (heads, arms and legs) available in general stores. Their products were not necessarily stylish, nor even beautiful, but must have delighted the hearts of the little girls who received them as cherished gifts, and who consequently played hard with the dolls and their wardrobes. In fact some of these wardrobes which have survived to the present day are equally treasured by their owners.

Be that as it may, not many original hats exist. If the doll collector wants her doll's charming face framed in a bonnet she may have to make a bonnet, or buy one.

For those collectors and costumers we have a few hints which might answer some important questions about what, **with** what, and how-to. In the following paragraphs you will find information concerning proper fit for bonnets, gauging the size of ties and bows, preference for types of bonnet suitable for a particular doll or a certain period, and selection of fabrics for bonnets in general.

CRITERIA FOR FITTING BONNETS.

Bonnets to look their best should be properly fitted to the doll and her costume, but it is sometimes difficult to know either what size to select, or to recognize factors which make for correct fit. The following suggestions should help in the selection of a pattern most nearly correct for a particular doll.

First, head circumferences are used to identify sizes. This measurement, a more reliable index of correct size, is taken with a measuring tape placed around the doll's head just above the ears and over the hair. Doll sizes (heights) cannot be related to hat sizes because of the great variation in head sizes and the type of body. (See chart below, which gives a comparison of these measurements between French and German dolls.)

CHART SHOWING COMPARISON OF FRENCH AND GERMAN DOLLS:*

German Bisque		French Bisque	
Head Circumference	**Height**	**Head Circumference**	**Height**
5in (12.7cm)	9in (22.9cm)	6½in (16.5cm)	9in (22.9cm)
6½in (16.5cm)	10½in (26.7cm) to 11in (27.9cm)	7in (17.8cm)	10in (25.4cm)
7in (17.8cm)	12½in (31.8cm)	7in (17.8cm) to 8in (20.3cm)	10½in (26.7cm) to 11in (27.9cm)
8in (20.3cm) to 8½in (21.6cm)	13in (33cm)	8½in (21.6cm) to 9in (22.9cm)	12in (30.5cm)
8½in (21.6cm) to 9in (22.9cm)	15in (38.1cm)	9in (22.9cm) to 9½in (24.2cm)	13in (33cm)
9in (22.9cm) to 9½in (24.2cm)	16in (40.6cm)	10in (25.4cm) to 10½in (26.7cm)	15in (38.1cm) to 16in (40.6cm)
10in (25.4cm) to 10½in (26.7cm)	18in (45.7cm) to 19in (48.3cm)	10½in (26.7cm) to 11in (27.9cm)	17in (43.2cm) to 20in (50.8cm)
10½in (26.7cm) to 11in (27.9cm)	20in (50.8cm)	11½in (29.2cm)	22in (55.9cm)
11in (27.9cm) to 11½in (29.2cm)	21in (53.3cm) to 22in (55.9cm)	12in (30.5cm) to 12½in (31.8cm)	24in (61cm)
12in (30.5cm) to 12½in (31.8cm)	23in (58.4cm) to 24in (61cm)	13in (33cm) to 13½in (34.3cm)	25in (63.5cm)
13in (33cm)	25in (63.5cm) to 26in (66cm)	13½in (34.3cm) to 14in (35.6cm)	26in (66cm)
13½in (34.3cm)	27in (68.6cm) to 28in (71.1cm)	14in (35.6cm) to 15in (38.1cm)	27in (68.6cm) to 28in (71.1cm)
14in (35.6cm) to 15in (38.1cm)	29in (73.7cm) to 30in (76.2cm)		
16in (40.6cm)	34in (86.4cm)		

*Please note: These figures were taken from various sources such as listings by makers of reproduction dolls, and by actual measurements of many dolls in these two categories. HOWEVER, these figures are not intended as authoritative data on doll sizes, but indicate clearly that it is not possible to select a bonnet pattern for a particular doll on the basis of its height. Head circumference will be a more reliable figure for a bonnet pattern.

We give an approximate scale relating height and circumference, but please keep in mind that these measurements must be correlated also to the doll being dressed. If there is any doubt about the correct size pattern for the doll being dressed (and before you spend several hours working on a bonnet which may be too large or too small) cut a CROWN of unbleached muslin and try it on the doll; then check the information which follows:

Bonnet-type hats should extend to the tip of the earlobe, and bonnets should be set back so that the doll's profile is clearly visible.

RIBBON TIES

While bows for **trim only** may be made of wide ribbon for decorative purposes, ties should be of a width in good scale to the size of the bonnet. For example, a bonnet for a 16in (40.6cm) tall doll (head circumference 10in [25.4cm]) would look best with ribbon ties about 5/8in (1.6cm) wide, while a bonnet for a 24in (61cm) tall doll (head circumference 14½in [36.9cm]) might look perfect with ties 1¼in (3.2cm) wide.

FABRICS

Fabrics selected must, of course, be suitable to the doll's costume. With cotton dresses, one might select from organdies, sateen, dull silks, lace, heavy cotton, lawn, percale and eyelet. With costumes of silk, there is a wide range of choice, dependent in part on the style of bonnet being made. Velvet is easy to work with when a buckram and wired frame is used, but may be much too heavy for a small-sized Normandy bonnet. Mob-type bonnets may be made of sheer silk if they are lined with organdy or muslin to give shape, and heavier silks would also work out satisfactorily.

The size of the bonnet may be the determining factor in selecting fabrics. A tiny bonnet would appear too bulky in a heavy-napped fabric, and would also be difficult to make. The reverse could be true for a very large hat made of sheer organdy or organza instead of a heavier cotton or silk to provide some stability. An exception to this statement is the use of sheer cottons for a style shirred on wire.

Eventually your good judgement will prevail and a particular bonnet will be judged as too bulky in velvet, a particular cotton may not be suitable for a Victorian bonnet, a fine silk too sheer for a wired brim, or one combination might be quite unsuitable for the dress with which it is to be worn.

To recapitulate, this brief review may be of help:

1. HATS WITH BUCKRAM AND WIRED FRAMES, use: velvet, heavy silk, heavy cotton or even sturdy wool.
2. HATS WITH HEAVY MUSLIN FRAMES, which in some cases are reinforced with wire and have a stiffener such as buckram or pellon, use: medium-weight silks such as Thai silk, silk broadcloth, cotton velvet or fine wool.
3. HATS WITH SHIRRED BRIMS, for the shirring, use: English net, very sheer silk or fine cotton.
4. MOB-TYPE BONNETS, either with or without reinforcement, use: sheer silks or medium-weight silks and cotton, or fine cottons.
5. FOR HAT LININGS, use: rather stiff but fine fabrics, such as organdy, which will hold out the full crown of a mob-type bonnet. For any buckram hats or bonnets, a lightweight to medium-weight fabric will serve.

POKE BONNET

Designed in two sizes for:
(1) 13½in (34.3cm) doll with 7½in (19.1cm) head circumference.
(2) 16in (40.6cm) doll with 10in (25.4cm) head circumference.

DESCRIPTION

This lovely little bonnet, prominent in the 1880s, has been designed with three pieces, BRIM, CROWN and BACK cut of muslin and reinforced with buckram or heavy pellon, and light milliners wire no. 21. Refer to chart on page 4 which suggests methods of determining correct size for particular dolls, and fabrics favorable to development of a firm but fashionable little doll bonnet.

MATERIALS REQUIRED, exclusive of trim:

Milliners wire no. 21
Stiffening: heavy pellon
Muslin, small pieces
Bonnet fabric

CUTTING INSTRUCTIONS

1. LINING: Cut of heavy muslin 1 each of BONNET BRIM, CROWN and BACK.
   STIFFENING: Using **heavy** pellon lining, cut 1 each of BONNET BRIM, CROWN and BACK. **Cut off seam** allowances of these pieces.
   BONNET FABRIC: Cut 1 BONNET BACK, 2 BONNET BRIMS and 1 BONNET CROWN, and true bias about 1in (2.5cm) by 18in (45.7cm).

HAT ASSEMBLY

(Please read section on GLUING, page 13, before starting to work.)

ASSEMBLY INSTRUCTIONS

2. LINING: Apply pellon pieces to corresponding sections, and machine-stitch. Using milliners wire no. 21, zigzag or sew by hand around outside edge of PELLON, allowing wire to extend about 2in (5.1cm) at ends of brim.

BONNET BRIM

3. Put corresponding fabric pieces of BRIM one on top of stiffening, and one underneath (a sandwich of stiffening between two layers of bonnet fabric) and baste lightly together along edges. Using the bias strip of bonnet fabric, lay on top of brim, and with zipper foot, machine-stitch as close to wire as possible. Roll bias over brim, turn under 1/4in (.65cm) and blindstitch to brim. Leave inside curved edge of brim unfinished.

BONNET CROWN

4. Place right side of bonnet fabric over muslin crown and machine-stitch 1/4in (.65cm) from edge (next to pellon, but do not stitch through it) along FRONT EDGE. Turn right sides out and press, smoothing seam line.

BONNET BACK

5. Using muslin back to which pellon has been sewn, turn down muslin seam allowance NOT including neck edge, and glue lightly in place, using a pin to distribute the edge smoothly and evenly. Place bonnet fabric wrong side on pellon, pin in place, and roll seam allowance over edge, glue or tack in place, again NOT including neck edge, but producing a neatly finished edge around front edge of crown.

ASSEMBLING BONNET BACK TO CROWN

6. Matching *s at center and ends of bonnet back and bonnet crown, pin in place first, and try to hold pieces in place firmly with fingers to prevent "traveling" as you hand-stitch securely with a blindstitch. With practice this seam line will be smooth and neat.

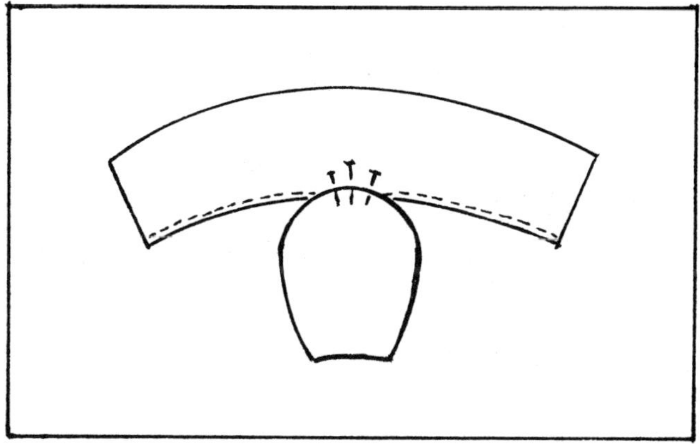

Illustration 3. Bonnet back set over crown, starting at center, at line of stitching.

In anticipation of slight problems on your first attempt to connect these two pieces, we suggest the following: Select six-strand embroidery floss to match bonnet fabric. Make a simple chain long enough to cover this seam, and tack carefully over the seam. This may also be done for purely decorative reasons, so never admit the reason; let it stand on its own merits!

NOTE: This braid may also be used on the stitching line for bias tape on top brim.

NECK EDGE

7. Using 1¼in (3.2cm) bias tape of bonnet fabric, pin to neck edge on the outside, right sides together and machine-stitch. LEAVE THIS WORK FOR THE MOMENT.

RUCHING: (See instructions for ruching, *Antique Children's Fashions, 1880-1900,* page 92.)

8. Attach ruching to top front edge of crown, ruching extending about 3/8in (.9cm) beyond crown edge.
   OPTIONAL: A second row may be attached on the underside of the crown, also extending about 3/8in (.9cm) beyond crown edge.

ATTACHING BRIM

9. Place brim on crown, matching raw edge to line shown on pattern. Determine where WIRE extensions fall, and cut two or three stitches of the bias binding and insert wires. After inserting wires, position brim correctly with center-fronts matching. Secure by stitching raw edge of brim to crown.

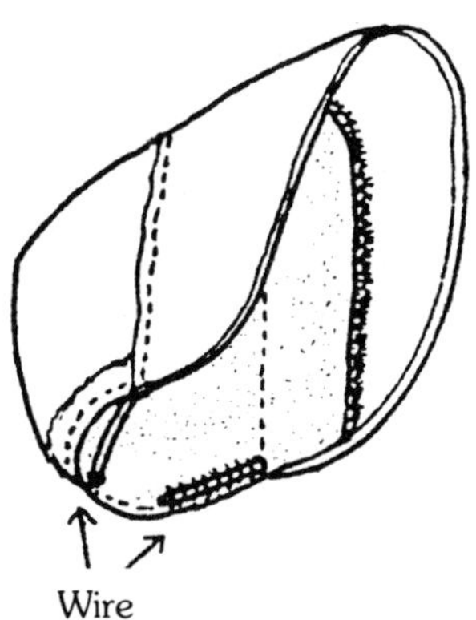

Illustration 4. Note bias partially completed, bonnet brim in place, with wires, one overcast in place, one still protruding.

On the INSIDE OF CROWN, use natural curve of wires at an angle which allows them to lie flat along edges of bonnet crown, and overcast in place. Fold bias tape over neck edge and stitch by hand, finishing neck edge and covering wire in one operation.

10. Using a 1in (2.5cm) piece of bias long enough to cover raw edge of brim, press edges to center. Lay this over the raw edge of brim and secure by tacking in place or by gluing.
ALTERNATE to this bias covering, consider one of the following:
a. Use KNOTTED RIBBON which is described in section on RIBBON TRIM.
b. Use SHIRRED RIBBON, as described on page 95, *Illustration 67, Antique Children's Fashions, 1880-1900.*
c. Weave a number of small flowers into a band and tack over edge.
d. Think of something all on your own.

THIS BONNET NOW LOOKS LIKE A BONNET, AND ALL THE REST OF THE WORK IS SHEER FUN.

OPTIONAL LINING

11. Optional lining is to be sewn in after all trimming is completed, thus covering all working stitches. Cut 1 crown and 1 brim from lining fabric, ON BIAS. Sew together as indicated in step 6. Turn down raw edges about 3/8in (.9cm) and press. Pin to inside of bonnet and hand-stitch in place, or glue lightly a few inches at a time.

BONNET TIES

12. Ties may be attached, using the following chart as a tentative guide for length of FINISHED ties, not including ribbon for bows at bonnet sides.
For 7½in (19.1cm) bonnet, use 7in (17.8cm) ties.
For 10in (25.4cm) bonnet, use 8in (20.3cm) ties.

LEFT: Illustration 5. 14½in (36.9cm) AT reproduction wearing a Poke bonnet with lace ruching and a large contrasting bow. *Photograph by Marty Ulseth.*

RIGHT: Illustration 6. 19in (48.3cm) Jumeau wearing a Poke bonnet showing an elaborate multi-looped bow. *Photograph by Marty Ulseth.*

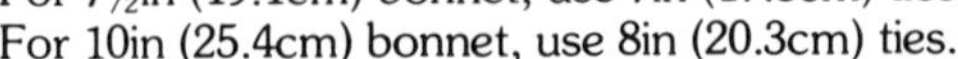

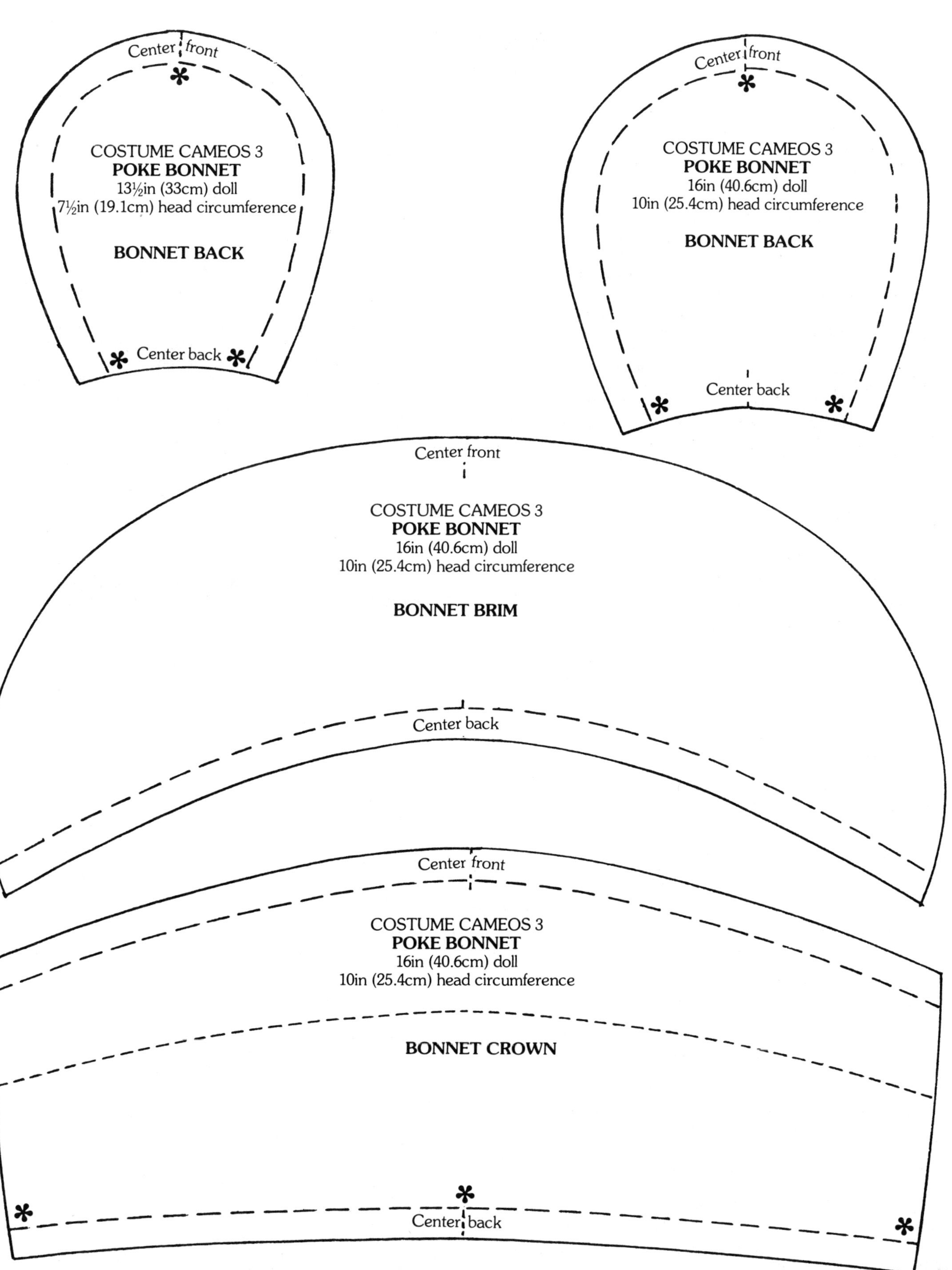
Center front
COSTUME CAMEOS 3
POKE BONNET
13½in (33cm) doll
7½in (19.1cm) head circumference
BONNET BACK
Center back
Center front
COSTUME CAMEOS 3
POKE BONNET
16in (40.6cm) doll
10in (25.4cm) head circumference
BONNET BACK
Center back
Center front
COSTUME CAMEOS 3
POKE BONNET
16in (40.6cm) doll
10in (25.4cm) head circumference
BONNET BRIM
Center back
Center front
COSTUME CAMEOS 3
POKE BONNET
16in (40.6cm) doll
10in (25.4cm) head circumference
BONNET CROWN
Center back

NORMANDY BONNET

(Adapted from *The Delineator*, April 1886)

The Normandy bonnet achieved much popularity for children's wear during the 1880s, a style derived by fashion artists from the headgear of French peasants from Normandy, a province in northwest France. The elaborate French headdresses were a veritable symphony of fine, often handmade lace, with frills and furbelows of all kinds, depending on the area in which they originated. Of course the children's bonnets were considerably simplified but were nonetheless charming. We are pleased to present here our adaptation of bonnets to doll size, using a simplified method of construction which will enable all would-be milliners to achieve success in making this bonnet.

This bonnet pattern has been designed for use with medium-weight fabrics with NO nap, so it would be unsuitable for velvet.

NOTE: Please refer to chart of bonnet sizes and related doll sizes in order to select a size for your doll which will be most accurate.

Two sizes of Normandy bonnets are presented in this book, as follows:
(1) For 16in (40.6cm) doll with 9½in (24.2cm) head circumference.
(2) For 20in (50.8cm) doll with 11½in (29.2cm) to 12in (30.5cm) head circumference.

CUTTING INSTRUCTIONS
1. LININGS.
   STIFFENER (used to give firm body to bonnet): **Heavy** pellon. Cut 1 BRIM, and cut off seam allowance.
   MUSLIN: Of muslin, organdy or cotton, cut 1 BRIM and 1 BODY.
   BONNET FABRIC: Cut 2 BRIMS, 1 BODY and a piece of true bias 1¼in (3.2cm) by 10in (25.4cm).
2. Baste **straight** edges of two BRIMS of bonnet right sides together. Baste pellon to muslin, centering carefully so that seam allowance is even all around. Place this on bonnet BRIMS and pin in place. Machine-stitch through muslin and bonnet fabric, along the outside edge of the pellon without catching pellon in the stitches. Separate the two bonnet BRIM pieces and turn one right side out. Press. Mark center backs with small safety pins.

COMPLETE BRIM
3. Try on doll, and lap over at centerback for comfortable fit, marking this point for a center back seam. Check edge of brim which should be even with earlobes. Form a seam at center back on fitting lines marked, by opening ends of brim and placing right sides together. Machine-stitch at point where fitting marks are, then press seams open.
   Flip cut edges upward, bring cut edges together and baste around inside edge of brim.

FINISHING BRIM INNER EDGE
4. Using a piece of bias strip about 1¼in (3.2cm) by 10in (25.4cm), lay along cut edge on inside of BRIM and hand- or machine-stitch. Turn to right side of brim and tack flat to brim. This edge will be covered by body of bonnet.

BODY OF BONNET
5. Place lining on body with marks on lining facing right side of bonnet fabric (so that they will be visible when fabric is turned) matching corresponding edges. Machine-stitch around body from *......* as shown on pattern. Turn right sides out and press. Turn edges of opening 1/4in (.65cm) and slipstitch closed.
   (NOTE: Markings for center back pleats are shown, and for area to be cartridge pleated.)

Illustration 7. This shows the development of the bow from positioning of first loops to completed bow.

SHAPING BODY
6. The large curved edge will be cartridge pleated to fit bonnet brim:
   FOR CARTRIDGE PLEATING:
   (1) Size 9½in (24.2cm) head circumference. Hand-stitch two rows of gathering stitches 1/8in (.31cm) long or slightly larger, with the rows 1/8in (.31cm) apart.
   (2) Size 11½in (29.2cm) to 12in (30.5cm) head circumference. Hand-stitch two rows of gathering stitches about 1/4in (.65cm) long, with rows 1/4in (.65cm) apart.
   Leave knots at each end so gathering can be pulled later.

PLACEMENT OF BODY
7. Note placement line for body as shown on pattern, for the size you are using. On bonnet brim mark this line by basting contrasting thread following line shown on pattern.
8. Place body on brim matching center back and pin. Continue to pin smoothly to the point where cartridge pleating starts. Blindstitch these sections on each side. **Re**adjust pleats to fit back area if necessary, and secure.

SECURING CARTRIDGE PLEATING
9. Pull gathering stitches to fit brim. Distribute gathering evenly and pin in place. Sew from the OUTSIDE, picking up the outside corner of each pleat starting at one side of bonnet. Sew about 1in (2.5cm) then start sewing from other side keeping stitch size equal on both sides. Continue working 1in (2.5cm) intervals at a time until reaching center front. (This is not so difficult as it sounds; just use two needles, one of which can be left dangling as you change from side to side.)

TRIM
10. RUCHING: Pleat insertion lace or edged lace (about 1/2in [1.3cm] wide) in 1/4in (.65cm) pleats. Sew at edge of BRIM on the underside, by hand.
    OPTIONAL: Place a second row of ruching around top edge of brim.

BOW TRIM
NOTE: Attractive bows elude many otherwise expert milliners so we have given instructions in detail; followed precisely, these instructions will produce a really nice old-fashioned bow, quite professional in appearance, and with total control of each loop of the bow. This type of bow is useful for many bonnets, and measurements given below may be easily altered to form a larger or smaller bow.

11. BOWS. For smaller size bonnet make this charming bow with multiple loops.
    RIBBON. 1 piece measuring 1/4in (.65cm) or 3/8in (.9cm) by 13in (33cm), cut as follows:
    Cut 1 piece 2½in (6.4cm) long.
    Cut 7 pieces, each 1½in (3.8cm) long.
    Bow is to be sewn to a small BASE (or band), 1/4in (.65cm) by 1in (2.5cm), which may be made of muslin folded twice to this size and stitched.
    SMALL LOOPS. Using the 1½in (3.8cm) pieces of ribbon fold each with cut edges together, and hand-stitch individually. Hand-gather across bottom of loop and pull in as tightly as possible. Secure.

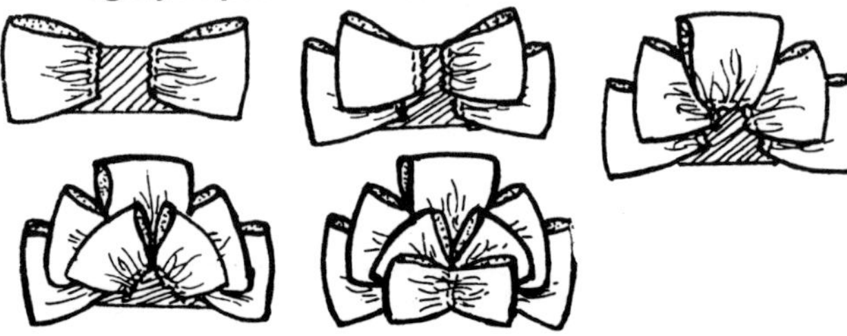

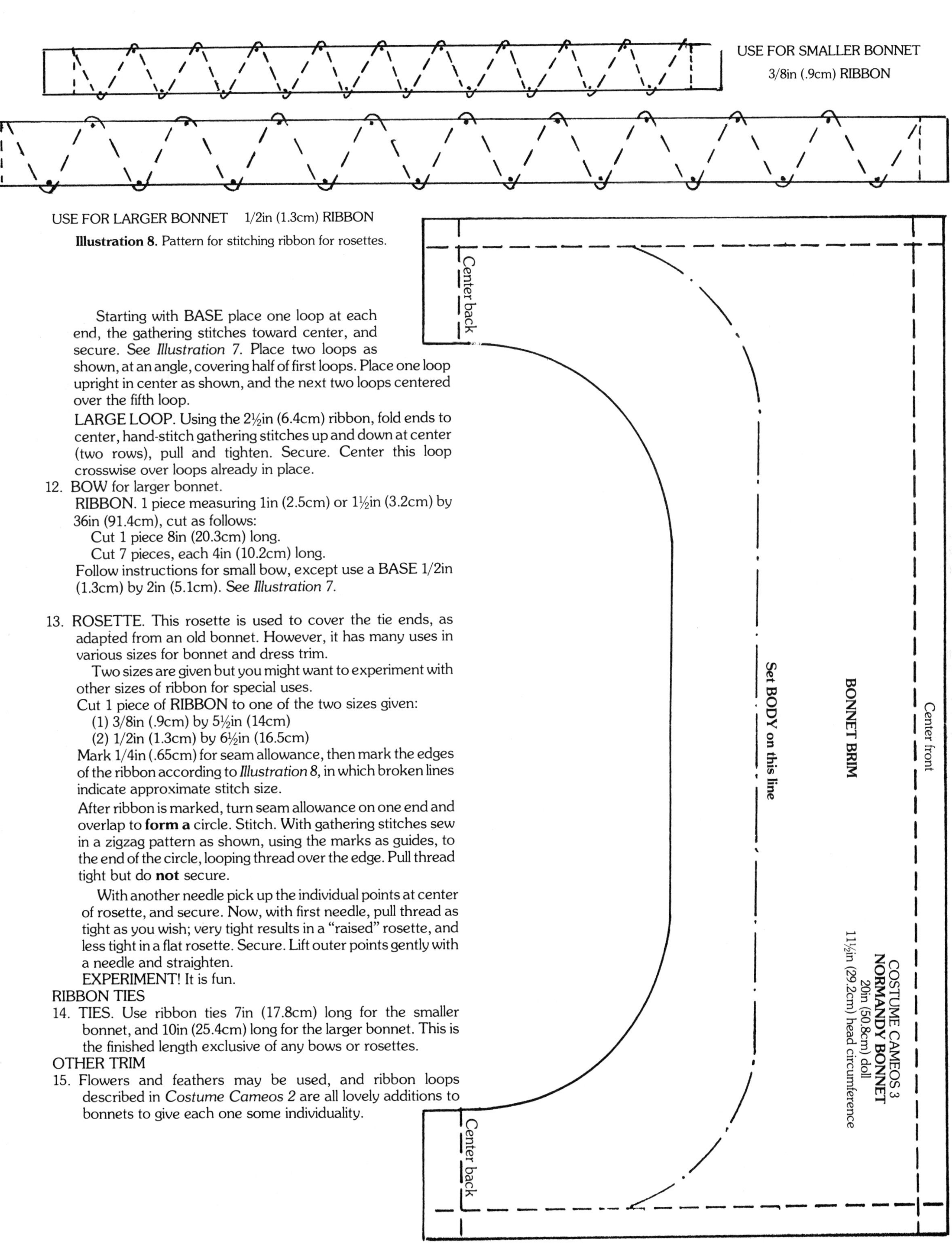

Illustration 8. Pattern for stitching ribbon for rosettes.

Starting with BASE place one loop at each end, the gathering stitches toward center, and secure. See *Illustration 7.* Place two loops as shown, at an angle, covering half of first loops. Place one loop upright in center as shown, and the next two loops centered over the fifth loop.

LARGE LOOP. Using the 2½in (6.4cm) ribbon, fold ends to center, hand-stitch gathering stitches up and down at center (two rows), pull and tighten. Secure. Center this loop crosswise over loops already in place.

12. BOW for larger bonnet.
RIBBON. 1 piece measuring 1in (2.5cm) or 1½in (3.2cm) by 36in (91.4cm), cut as follows:
Cut 1 piece 8in (20.3cm) long.
Cut 7 pieces, each 4in (10.2cm) long.
Follow instructions for small bow, except use a BASE 1/2in (1.3cm) by 2in (5.1cm). See *Illustration 7.*

13. ROSETTE. This rosette is used to cover the tie ends, as adapted from an old bonnet. However, it has many uses in various sizes for bonnet and dress trim.

Two sizes are given but you might want to experiment with other sizes of ribbon for special uses.
Cut 1 piece of RIBBON to one of the two sizes given:
(1) 3/8in (.9cm) by 5½in (14cm)
(2) 1/2in (1.3cm) by 6½in (16.5cm)
Mark 1/4in (.65cm) for seam allowance, then mark the edges of the ribbon according to *Illustration 8,* in which broken lines indicate approximate stitch size.

After ribbon is marked, turn seam allowance on one end and overlap to **form a** circle. Stitch. With gathering stitches sew in a zigzag pattern as shown, using the marks as guides, to the end of the circle, looping thread over the edge. Pull thread tight but do **not** secure.

With another needle pick up the individual points at center of rosette, and secure. Now, with first needle, pull thread as tight as you wish; very tight results in a "raised" rosette, and less tight in a flat rosette. Secure. Lift outer points gently with a needle and straighten.
EXPERIMENT! It is fun.

RIBBON TIES
14. TIES. Use ribbon ties 7in (17.8cm) long for the smaller bonnet, and 10in (25.4cm) long for the larger bonnet. This is the finished length exclusive of any bows or rosettes.

OTHER TRIM
15. Flowers and feathers may be used, and ribbon loops described in *Costume Cameos 2* are all lovely additions to bonnets to give each one some individuality.

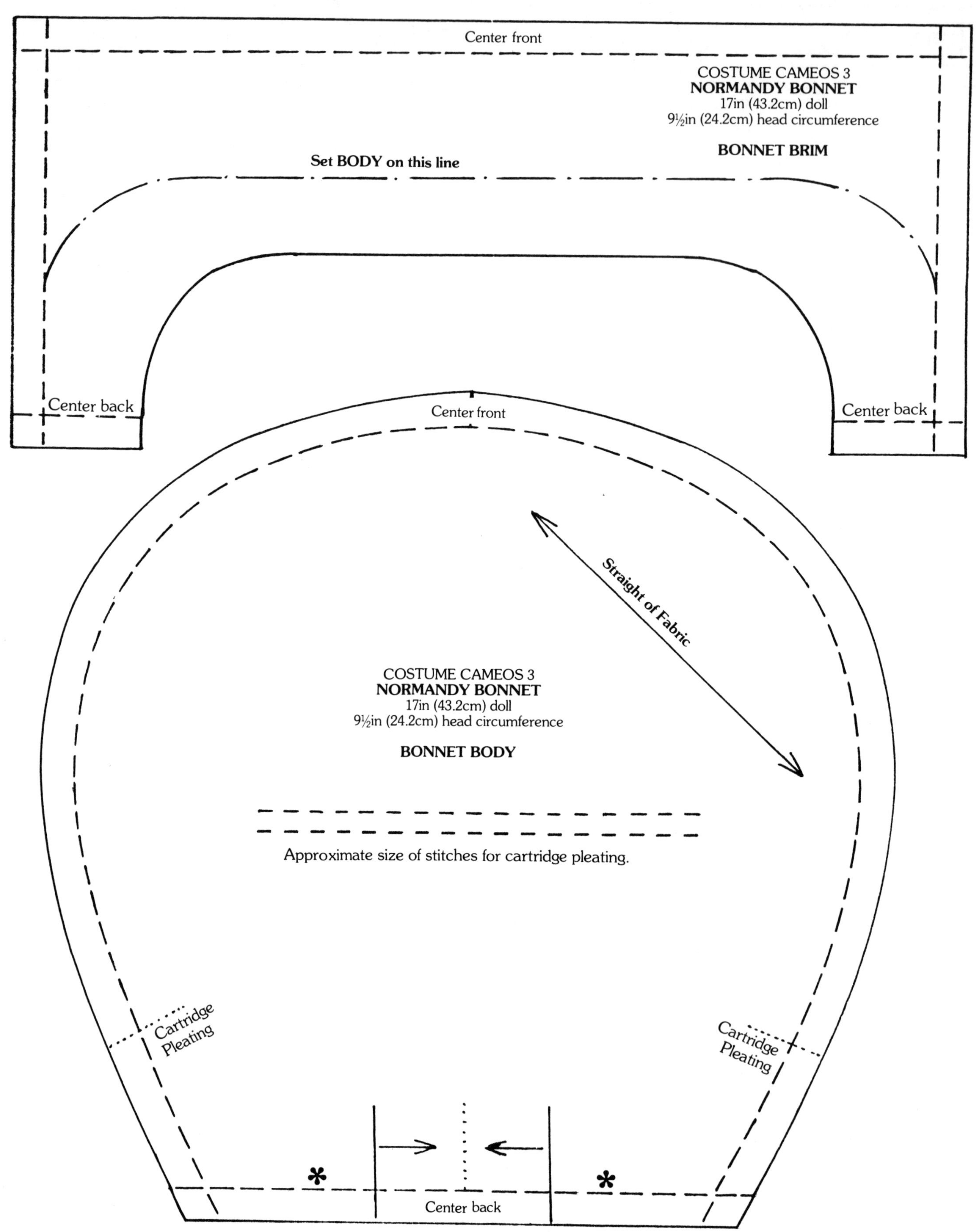

Center front
COSTUME CAMEOS 3
NORMANDY BONNET
17in (43.2cm) doll
9½in (24.2cm) head circumference
BONNET BRIM
Set BODY on this line
Center back
Center back
Center front
Straight of Fabric
COSTUME CAMEOS 3
NORMANDY BONNET
17in (43.2cm) doll
9½in (24.2cm) head circumference
BONNET BODY
Approximate size of stitches for cartridge pleating.
Cartridge Pleating
Cartridge Pleating
*
*
Center back

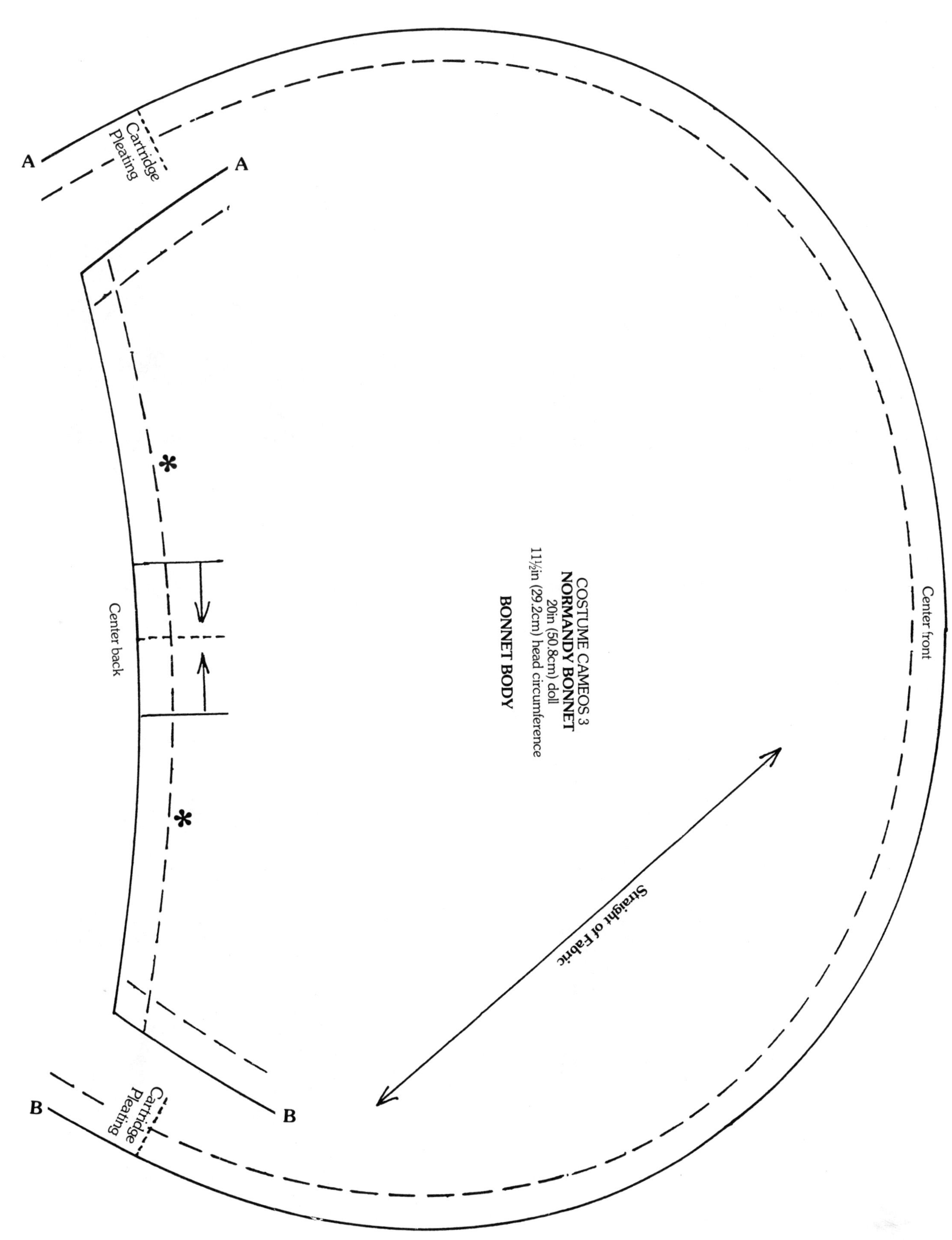

A
A
Cartridge Pleating
B
B
Cartridge Pleating
Center back
Center front
*
*
COSTUME CAMEOS 3
NORMANDY BONNET
20in (50.8cm) doll
11½in (29.2cm) head circumference
BONNET BODY
Straight of Fabric

Illustration 9. 20in (50.8cm) long-faced Jumeau wearing a Normandy bonnet trimmed with lace ruching and small velour flowers. *Photograph by Marty Ulseth.*

Illustration 10. 17in (43.2cm) unmarked turned-head German bisque wearing a Normandy bonnet with ruching at the brim, a multi-looped bow and flowers. *Photograph by Marty Ulseth.*

Illustration 11. 20in (50.8cm) long-faced Jumeau wearing a Normandy bonnet featuring ruching around brim, a large ribbon bow and velour flowers. *Photograph by Marty Ulseth.*

Illustration 12. 17in (43.2cm) unmarked turned-head German bisque wearing a Normandy bonnet with full ruching, tiny handmade roses and a pert feather. *Photograph by Marty Ulseth.*

GLUING TECHNIQUES

Much tiresome labor may be avoided in making bonnets by gluing in certain phases of construction, but improper techniques may ruin fabrics by bleeding through, glue improperly applied might leave lumpy areas, and most important of all, once gluing is done it is almost irreversible. Unlike sewing, it cannot be removed stitch by stitch, and a serious error could result in the necessity of starting all over again.

However do not be frightened away from a time-saver such as gluing, just be careful, plan a little, practice, and keep in mind the following suggestions:

1. Use white glue (Elmer's or Sobo).
2. Use the least possible amount of glue to do a good job.
3. When applying glue, place little beads of glue along the two edges to be joined (tiny beads, as shown in *Illustration 13*). Using a hat pin, smooth over those little globules into a smooth, thin layer which will spread out to about 1/4in (.65cm).
4. Allow glue to set, usually about 1 minute.
5. Keep in mind that it is very difficult to sew through glued fabrics, so be selective of the areas in which you use glue.
6. If you are using a fabric which is lightweight and might allow glue to bleed through, apply a thin layer of glue on the area which will later be glued, using the method described in step 3. Let this dry, then apply again as directed. **Do** experiment first on the fabric you plan to use to be certain this can be done safely.

NOTE: If your white glue is rather thick, it may be diluted with a little water.

Illustration 13.

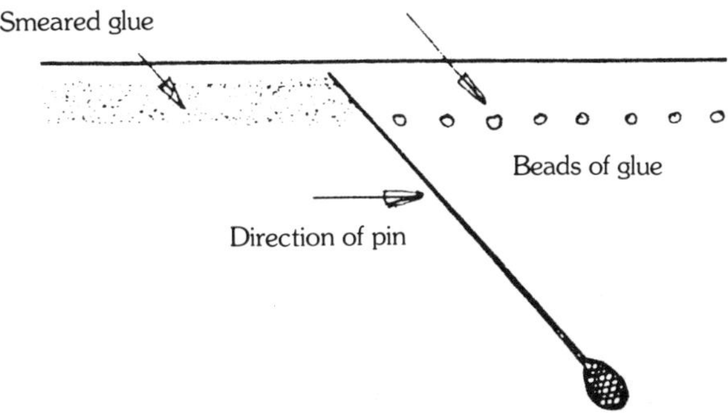

Attach the two glued pieces, applying pressure gently.

Ruching is gathered or pleated lace, ribbon or fabric in a width suitable for trimming, used at neck edges, cuffs, and in this case, as trim on bonnets. For bonnet trim it is applied at the edge of the crown next to the doll's head, or a double row of ruching may be used. It will look attractive at the outer edge of the brim, or across the top of the crown when no brim is used. The width will vary according to the size of the garment or bonnet, or the area on which it is to be used.

Ruching may be made of edged lace, of insertion lace, of fine silk, or ribbon. Insertion lace will make very attractive ruching, and provides a use for insertion which many of us have, but have been unable to use effectively.

Some of the following ideas may stir your imagination to even better ideas for using the materials which you have at hand:

1. Using insertion or edged lace, pleat at 1/4in (.65cm) intervals with pleats touching, to the length required. Do not press.
2. Adding color to ruching.
   a. Before pleating, overcast edge of lace with two or three strands of embroidery floss in color desired. When pleated this makes a dainty colored edge.
   b. Before pleating, run embroidery thread in and out of holes in lace (a very fast method) or overcast along edge of lace, catching only a single thread with each stitch.
   c. On coarse lace use a fine zigzag in color to add contrast and interest.
   d. Experiment with a fine-tipped marking pen to color the edging of fine lace, but do not tell anyone you did it!
3. RIBBON RUCHING. Follow instructions in step 1 for pleating. Ribbon will make a rather stiff ruching and does not have the fluffy charm of lace, but it is attractive when used on bonnet edges, and for more formal trim on fashion dresses, particularly on cuffs and skirts, and it may add just the touch you need.

4. SKIRT RUFFLE, with finished edges, no hemming required. Cut a bias ruffle of lightweight silk about 2½in (6.4cm) wide, and approximately twice the length of the area to be trimmed. Fold and baste raw edges together. Do not press. Turn right side out, forming a long tube. Roll seam about 3/8in (.9cm) toward back. On the fold thus formed, machine- or hand-stitch two rows of gathering stitches, the first row 1/8in (.31cm) from fold, the second row on fold, gathering as needed for trim. Experiment with different widths to achieve suitable width for garment to be trimmed. (NOTE: This method avoids any hemming and provides two finished edges.)
5. SKIRT RUFFLE, as above, except forming a 1/4in (.65cm) heading. Following instructions in step 4, except: roll seam 5/8in (1.6cm), machine- or hand-stitch two rows of gathering stitches, the first row 3/8in (.9cm) from fold, the second row 1/4in (.65cm) from fold, thus forming a 1/4in (.65cm) heading.
6. SKIRT RUFFLE of double fabric with cut edges covered by ribbon or insertion.

Decide on width of finished ruffle, double this amount and add 1/2in (1.3cm) for seam allowance (for a 1½in [3.8cm] finished ruffle, measurements as follows: two x 1½in [5.1cm x 3.8cm] = 3in [7.6cm] and 1/2in [1.3cm] for seam, 3½in [8.9cm]).

Fold with cut edges together, baste and machine- or hand-stitch two rows of gathering stitches, first row 1/4in (.65cm) from cut edge, the second row 1/8in (.31cm) from edge. Pull gathering stitches to fit area to be trimmed and tack in place. Cover cut edge with narrow insertion or narrow ribbon, thus adding color and texture while covering a cut edge.

Illustration 14.

Trim for adult doll clothing, particularly for fashion dolls, is simple, effective, colorful (a perfect match when made from self-fabric) and you have the making at hand.

FRINGED RUFFLE

1. RUFFLE WITHOUT HEADING: Cut of self-fabric 7/8in (2.2cm) strips in length required (about two times the area to be trimmed).

   RUFFLE WITH HEADING: Cut of self-fabric 1⅛in (2.8cm) strips in length required (about two times the area to be trimmed).

2. Using an interesting contrasting color of thread, zigzag a very narrow stitch 1/4in (.65cm) to 3/8in (.9cm) from edge to be fringed.

3. RUFFLE WITHOUT HEADING: Mark 3/8in (.9cm) from other cut edge, press fabric to wrong side. With same color as that used for zigzagging, machine-stitch one row of gathering stitches as close to fold as possible, and one row 1/8in (.31cm) from fold.

   RUFFLE WITH HEADING: Mark 1/2in (1.3cm) from other cut edge, press fabric to wrong side. With same color as that used for zigzagging, machine-stitch one row of gathering stitches 3/8in (.9cm) from fold, and one row 1/4in (.65cm) from fold.

4. On edge with zigzag clip from cut edge up to zigzag stitch about every 10in (25.4cm) to facilitate fringing process.

5. Pull threads in area between clipping, up to zigzag stitch.

6. Pull gathering stitches gently and apply to area to be trimmed. Tack in place. A lovely trim is formed when fringing is applied in two matching rows of scallops.

FRINGING RIBBON ENDS

7. For sash ends, cut selvage off both sides of ribbon about 1/4in (.65cm) from ends and pull threads to form fringe.

GLIMPSES of the PAST

Early Autumn Toilettes
for Young Folks.
1899